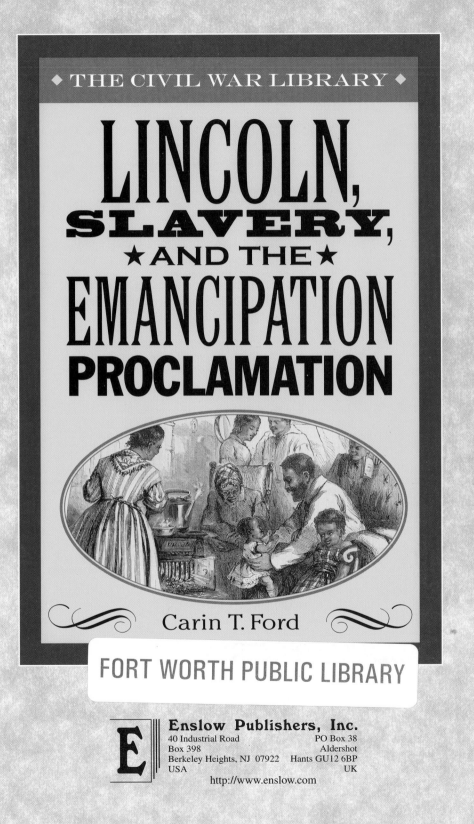

◆ THE CIVIL WAR LIBRARY ◆

LINCOLN, SLAVERY, ★AND THE★ EMANCIPATION PROCLAMATION

Carin T. Ford

E **Enslow Publishers, Inc.**

40 Industrial Road   PO Box 38
Box 398   Aldershot
Berkeley Heights, NJ 07922   Hants GU12 6BP
USA   UK

http://www.enslow.com

Library of Congress Cataloging-in-Publication Data

Ford, Carin T.
   Lincoln, slavery, and the Emancipation Proclamation / Carin T. Ford.
      v. cm. — (The Civil War library)
   Includes bibliographical references and index.
      Contents: Slavery takes root—The battle over slavery—A nation torn apart—Taking action—Letting freedom ring—Timeline.
   ISBN 0-7660-2252-8 (hardcover)
      1. Lincoln, Abraham, 1809–1865—Views on slavery—Juvenile literature. 2. Slavery—United States—History—Juvenile literature. 3. Slaves—Emancipation—United States—Juvenile literature.
4. United States. President (1861–1865 : Lincoln). Emancipation Proclamation—Juvenile literature.
5. United States—Politics and government—1861–1865—Juvenile literature. [1. Slavery—History.
2. Emancipation Proclamation. 3. United States—Politics and government—1861–1865. 4. African Americans—History. 5. Lincoln, Abraham, 1809–1865.] I. Title.
   E457.2.F68   2004
   973.7'112—dc22   2003013720

Printed in the United States of America

10 9 8 7 6 5 4 3 2

To Our Readers: We have done our best to make sure all Internet Addresses in this book were active and appropriate when we went to press. However, the author and the publisher have no control over and assume no liability for the material available on those Internet sites or on other Web sites they may link to. Any comments or suggestions can be sent by e-mail to comments@enslow.com or to the address on the back cover.

Every effort has been made to locate all copyright holders of material used in this book. If any errors or omissions have occurred, corrections will be made in future editions of this book.

Illustration Credits: *Authentic Civil War Illustrations*, Dover Publications, Inc., 1995, pp. 2, 21; © Corel Corporation, pp. 15, 29B, 39; Dover Publications, Inc., pp. 2, 21; Enslow Publishers, Inc., maps pp. 14, 20, 40TC; Hemera Technologies, Inc. 1997–2000, p. 40; Library of Congress, pp. 1 (inset), 4–5 (background), 5 (inset), 6B, 7, 8, 8 (inset), 9T, 9B, 11T, 11B, 12 (Liberator), 12–13C, 16T, 16B, 17T, 17C, 18 (background), 18 (inset), 19T, 19B, 20L, 22L, 22–23C, 23T, 24 (background), 24 (inset), 25T, 25B, 26, 27T, 27B, 28, 29T, 30, 31 (inset), 32L, 32C, 34B, 35T, 36, 37, 38T, 38C, 38B, 40TL, 40TR, 41TL, 41TR, 41C, 41BR, 42, 43T; National Archives and Records Administration, pp. 12 (portrait TL), 19C, 34T, 40B, 41BL, 43B; North Wind Picture Archives, pp. 6T, 10 (background), 10 (inset), 13T; Roy Meredith, *Mr. Lincoln's Camera Man*, 2nd Rev. Ed., Dover Publications, Inc., 1974, p. 35B; Photograph and Prints Division, Schomberg Center for Research in Black Culture, pp. 31 (background), 33.

Cover Illustration: Inset, Library of Congress. All other cover photos courtesy of the following: Library of Congress; National Archives; Photos.com; Enslow Publishers, Inc.; with the exception of: Song Book, Courtesy National Park Service, Museum Management Program and Gettysburg National Military Park, catalog number GETT31374, www.cr.nps.gov/museum/exhibits/gettex/music2.htm; Patriotic Cover, Courtesy National Park Service, Museum Management Program and Gettysburg National Military Park, catalog number GETT27703, www.cr.nps.gov/museum/exhibits/gettex/write5.htm; Drum carried by Mozart Regiment, Courtesy National Park Service, Museum Management Program and Gettysburg National Military Park, catalog number GETT32847, www.cr.nps.gov/museum/exhibits/gettex/music3.htm; US Flag, Courtesy National Park Service, Museum Management Program and Manassas National Battlefield Park, catalog number MANA979, www.cr.nps.gov/museum/exhibits/flags/mana2.htm.

TABLE OF CONTENTS

CHAPTER ONE

SLAVERY TAKES ROOT

"If slavery is not wrong, nothing is wrong."[1] When Abraham Lincoln wrote these words, Americans were bitterly divided over slavery. For nearly 250 years, black slaves had worked hard on farms and plantations, mainly in the South. Slaves were bought and sold like property. Their owners did not pay them for their work. Many slaves

Most slaves worked in the South on the large cotton plantations where two-thirds of the world's cotton was grown.

were beaten with whips and given little food or clothing.

The businesses, factories, and small farms of the North did not need slave labor, and many Northerners had come to believe that slavery was wrong. They wanted to put an end to it.

Beatings and whippings left many slaves crippled.

The large plantations of the South depended on the work of slaves, and most

Southerners wanted to keep slavery. As president, Lincoln did more than anyone before him to free the 4 million black slaves from their chains.

Lincoln was born February 12, 1809, near Hodgenville, Kentucky. He came from a poor family of pioneers. They moved often, throughout the West.

Lincoln grew up near the Cumberland Trail, which ran from Louisville, Kentucky, to Nashville, Tennessee. Pioneers, preachers, and peddlers made their way along the trail. There were also slaves, tied together by the hands and feet, traveling on the trail. This is probably where young Abraham Lincoln saw slaves for the first time.[2]

The first African slaves were brought to America in 1619. Traders from Europe made a lot of money selling slaves. Men, women, and children were kidnapped in Africa, chained, and shipped across the Atlantic Ocean to America. Millions died on the long journey across the sea. Through the years,

"There was nothing to be heard but the rattling of chains, smacking of whips, and the groans and cries of our fellow men," said Ottobah Cugoano, recalling his time on a slave ship.[3]

Abraham had very little schooling, but he loved to read. Still, farm chores took up most of his time.

the number of slaves in America grew slowly. That suddenly changed when Eli Whitney invented the cotton gin in 1793. The machine removed the seeds from the cotton. With a machine doing the work instead of a person, farmers could now clean fifty times more cotton each day.

Slaves were often chained together so they could not escape.

Southern farmers could make a great deal of money selling this crop. Many of them quickly switched to growing cotton. More slaves than ever were needed to work in the fields, planting and picking the cotton.

A plantation was a large farm in the South where crops such as cotton were grown.

By 1830, the number of slaves had climbed to more than 2 million, and slavery had become a part of life in the United States.[4]

CHAPTER TWO

THE BATTLE ★OVER★ SLAVERY

In 1828, Lincoln traveled on a flatboat down the Mississippi River to New Orleans, Louisiana. The boat was carrying farm products to market. As legend tells the story, Lincoln, age nineteen, now got a closer look at slavery. Slaves in chains were being whipped. Black men, women, and children were being sold like cattle at auctions. Lincoln began to feel a deep hatred of slavery.[1]

Lincoln was not the only one in the country who felt strongly about slavery. Mostly in the North, there were many people who wanted to abolish—or put an end to—slavery. They were called abolitionists.

William Lloyd Garrison was an abolitionist who published an antislavery newspaper. He called it *The Liberator*. The word *liberate* means "to set free."

"I will not retreat a single inch—*and I will be heard*," wrote Garrison in the newspaper's first issue.[2] Garrison's voice was heard for the next thirty-five years. He also spread his views by helping form

Traveling down the Mississippi gave Lincoln a new view of life in the South.

Lincoln was shocked the first time he saw slaves for sale.

FOR SALE

A likely yo

NEGRO

William Lloyd Garrison's message in *The Liberator* came through loud and clear: Slavery should be stopped immediately.

the American Anti-Slavery Society in 1833. Members of the society gave speeches and wrote newspaper and magazine articles calling for an end to slavery.

Many people in the South were angry about these antislavery groups. Southerners asked the Northern lawmakers to put a stop to them. People in the South did not want slavery to end. The cotton industry needed slaves.

Lincoln was a member of the Illinois House of Representatives at this time. In 1837, Illinois's lawmakers voted to stop antislavery activity. Only six lawmakers voted in favor of the abolitionists. Lincoln was one of them. He wrote that slavery was based on "injustice and bad policy."[3] Still, he said that Congress did not have the power to end slavery in states where it

CRADLE OF
LIBERTY.

WORCESTER, SC

already existed. It was the first time Lincoln spoke out in public against slavery. But it was far from his last.

After his term in the Illinois Congress ended, Lincoln returned to his law practice. In 1841, Lincoln was the lawyer for a woman who had been sold into slavery in Illinois. He won her freedom

As a lawyer, Lincoln was known as an honest man and a good speaker.

All over the North, abolitionists like Wendell Phillips, above, told crowds of people about the horrors of slavery.

13

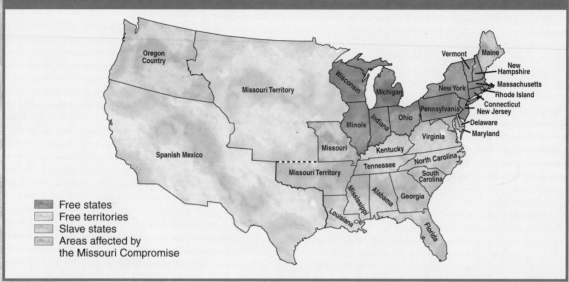

Oregon Country

Missouri Territory

Spanish Mexico

Missouri Territory

Wisconsin

Michigan

Illinois

Indiana

Ohio

Missouri

Kentucky

Tennessee

Mississippi

Alabama

Georgia

Louisiana

Florida

Vermont

Maine

New York

New Hampshire

Massachusetts

Rhode Island

Connecticut

New Jersey

Pennsylvania

Delaware

Maryland

Virginia

North Carolina

South Carolina

Free states
Free territories
Slave states
Areas affected by
the Missouri Compromise

by arguing that Illinois was not a slave state, so a person could not be bought or sold there.

Lincoln was elected for a two-year term in the United States Congress. As a congressman, from 1847 to 1849, he was rather quiet on the issue of slavery. At one point, he said that he would suggest a law to free the slaves in Washington, D.C., but he did not follow through on this.

In 1820, the Missouri Compromise allowed Maine to enter the Union as a free state and said Missouri would be a slave state. That kept an equal number of slaves states and free states.

Congress was working hard to satisfy both the

abolitionists of the North and the slave owners of the South. The Compromise of 1850 brought in California as a free state and banned the slave trade in the District of Columbia (although slavery was still allowed there). For the South, it made stricter punishments for anyone helping a runaway slave. Neither the North nor the South thought the Compromise of 1850 was fair.

When Lincoln ran for a seat in the U.S. Senate in 1858, slavery was an important issue to the voters. Even more new territories and states were being settled in the West. Should slavery be allowed in these areas?

Many people were moving out west in the mid-1800s. Lincoln did not think slavery should be allowed in the new parts of the country.

Lincoln believed the answer was no. He said it could stay in the states where it already existed, but he thought that over time, slavery would come to an end by itself.

The man Lincoln was running against for the Senate was Stephen A. Douglas. Lincoln and Douglas argued often about slavery. In Douglas's opinion, the people in each area should decide for themselves whether or not to allow slavery.

Stephen A. Douglas was small but powerful. He was known as "The Little Giant."[4]

Lincoln did not agree. He called slavery "the disease of the entire nation."[5] He feared that Douglas's plan would spread slavery throughout the American West.

Lincoln always worried that slavery might split the country in two. In a famous speech, he used a quote from the Bible: "A house divided against itself cannot stand." He went on to say that the country "will become all one thing, or all the other."[6] He was saying that one day, the whole country would either abolish slavery or allow it.

Lincoln lost the election to Douglas, yet his

speeches against slavery were remembered.

In 1860, Lincoln ran for president. He did not win many votes in the Southern slave states. The votes for Lincoln came from the eighteen free states. Lincoln's problems began immediately after he won the election. Southerners knew that he was against the spread of slavery. They were afraid that as president he would try to get rid of slavery in the whole country. So they decided to take action.

The country would not last as "half slave and half free," said Lincoln.[7]

CHAPTER THREE

A NATION TORN APART

South Carolina was the first state to break away—or secede—from the United States in December 1860. Six more southern states (Mississippi, Florida, Alabama, Georgia, Louisiana, and Texas) soon followed. They formed their own country—the Confederate States of America—with its own government.

Lincoln was sworn in as the sixteenth president of the United States on March 4, 1861. President Lincoln did not want the nation torn apart. "Can this country be saved?" he had asked before taking office. "If it can, I will consider myself one of the happiest men in the world if I can help to save it."[1]

Jefferson Davis became president of the Confederate States on February 18, 1861, in Montgomery, Alabama.

Fighting broke out when Confederate soldiers in South Carolina attacked Fort Sumter on April 12, 1861. The fort belonged to the U.S. government. With few men or supplies, it was forced to surrender. After this, four more states (Virginia, Arkansas, North Carolina, and Tennessee) seceded from the United States, bringing the total of Confederate States to eleven.

JEFFERSON DAVIS

The bombing of Fort Sumter in Charleston, South Carolina, marked the start of the Civil War.

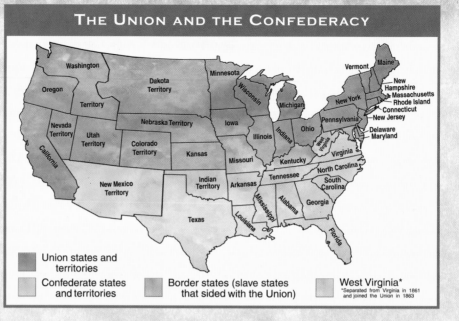

THE UNION AND THE CONFEDERACY

Union states and territories

Confederate states and territories

Border states (slave states that sided with the Union)

West Virginia*
*Separated from Virginia in 1861 and joined the Union in 1863

Although he had hoped to avoid war, Lincoln now called for 75,000 men to join the Union army. The Civil War had begun.

From the start, Lincoln said the war was being fought to save the country, not to destroy slavery. "If I could save the Union without freeing

When Lincoln was elected, he said that he did not plan to interfere with slavery in the slave states.

any slave I would do it, and if I could save it by freeing all the slaves I would do it; . . . What I do about slavery, and the colored race," he wrote, "I do because it helps to save the Union."[2]

Lincoln believed that most Union soldiers were fighting to save their country. He did not think they would be willing to risk their lives to free the slaves.[3]

Still, the growing number of abolitionists in the North wanted Lincoln to end slavery right away. Lincoln believed slavery was wrong—but he also believed in upholding the laws of the United States. He was not sure the U.S. Constitution gave him the power to abolish slavery. It had always been a matter that each state decided for itself.

Lincoln was also worried about Kentucky, Missouri, Maryland, and Delaware. These states were on the border of the North and the South. They were loyal to the Union—but they allowed slavery. Would they join the Confederacy if Lincoln got rid of slavery?

Kentucky led the way to the West, as well as to the heart of the Confederacy. "I think to lose Kentucky is nearly the same as to lose the whole game," Lincoln said.[4]

WHO'S WHO IN
THE CIVIL WAR

❖ The North was also known as the Union, or the United States. The people there were often called Yankees.

❖ The South was called the Confederacy, or the Confederate States. During the war, Southerners were also called Rebels or Johnny Reb.

After a year of fighting, the North had lost a lot of men and was not winning many battles. "Things had gone on from bad to worse," said Lincoln.[5] He decided the time had come to free the slaves. He said it was a "military necessity" if he hoped to put the country back together.[6]

When asked to do away with slavery, Lincoln said, "I can assure you, that the subject is on my mind, by day and night, more than any other."[7]

Lincoln believed that freeing—or emancipating—the slaves would hurt the South. For one thing, the South's cotton fields would lose most of its workers if there were no slaves. For another, these former slaves would be able to join the Union army. This would help the North.

One morning in June 1862, Lincoln visited the telegraph office of the War Department. The telegraph was a machine for sending messages. It was used in the days before the telephone was invented. Lincoln wanted to see the reports on how the Union

People in the North were not happy with the way the war was going. The first Battle of Bull Run was one of the bad Union losses.

Some runaway slaves stayed with the army. They were called "contraband of war." This meant they were like goods taken from the enemy. Now they belonged to the North.

army was doing. It was a quiet place, and Lincoln knew he could work there without being disturbed. Thomas T. Eckert was the head of the office. He said Lincoln came in one day and asked for a piece of paper "to write something special."[8]

Lincoln was about to begin writing the Emancipation Proclamation. *Emancipation* means freedom. A *proclamation* is a public announcement.

CHAPTER FOUR

TAKING ACTION

E ckert remembered the day Lincoln began writing this paper: "He would look out the window a while and then put his pen to paper, but he did not write much at once," Eckert said. "He would study between times and when he had made up his mind he would put down a line or two, and then sit quiet for a few minutes."[1]

That day, when Lincoln was finished, he handed Eckert the paper and asked him to hold on to it. Lincoln had not filled even one sheet.

There were times when Lincoln wrote only a couple of lines. Thomas Eckert saw some question marks on the edges of the papers.[2]

For the next few weeks, Lincoln came to the telegraph office each day. Eckert would take out the papers, which he kept in a locked desk, and hand them to the president.

Lincoln did not tell Eckert what he was working on until he had finished. Then Lincoln explained that he was freeing the slaves in the South. He said this would end the war more quickly.

Thomas Eckert and Abraham Lincoln became friendly during the president's many visits to the telegraph office. Eckert later became Assistant Secretary of War.

Lincoln's Emancipation Proclamation stated that all the slaves in the rebelling states were being set free.[3]

25

The Emancipation Proclamation also said that blacks would be allowed to join the U.S. army and navy.

In July 1862, Lincoln asked other lawmakers for advice about the Emancipation Proclamation. Some liked it. Others worried that there were many Northerners who might be upset. Even though most people in the North believed slavery was wrong, many of them

This is an early draft of Lincoln's Emancipation Proclamation.

Lincoln read his proclamation to his advisers.

26

In pursuance of the sixth section of the act of congress entitled "An act to suppress insurrection and to punish treason and rebellion, to seize and confiscate property of rebels, and for other purposes" Approved July 17. 1862, and which act, and the joint Resolution explanatory thereof, are herewith published, I, Abraham Lincoln, President of the United States, do hereby proclaim to, and warn all persons within the contemplation of said sixth section to cease participating in, and

did not think black people were equal to whites. They did not think blacks should have the same rights as white people, and they did not want the 4 million African-American slaves to be set free.

Lincoln said he was "afraid that half the officers [in the Union army] would fling down their arms" and refuse to fight when they heard about his plan to free the slaves.[4]

Secretary of State William H. Seward was pleased with the proclamation. But he told Lincoln not to issue it right away. The people in the North were not happy about how the war was going. The Union army had not won an important battle in a long while. Seward thought it might look as if Lincoln had written the Emancipation Proclamation just so African Americans could help fight in the Union army.

Secretary of State William H. Seward did not want Lincoln's paper to be misunderstood.

27

The Battle of Antietam was the victory Lincoln was waiting for.

Seward told Lincoln to wait until the North had won a big battle.[5] Lincoln agreed, and he waited. Finally, on September 17, 1862, the battle of Antietam took place near Sharpsburg, Maryland. It was the bloodiest single day of fighting in American history. More than 23,000 men were killed or wounded. The battle was terrible, but it was a victory for the North.

Five days later, on September 22, 1862, Lincoln published a draft of his proclamation—called the Preliminary Emancipation Proclamation.

Lincoln gave a warning to the Confederate States: If they did not come back into the Union by January 1, 1863, the Emancipation Proclamation would take effect, freeing all the slaves in the rebelling Southern states.

Lincoln visited the battlefield at Antietam.

◆ THE PRESIDENT'S WARTIME POWER ◆

Could President Lincoln end slavery without disobeying the U.S. Constitution? As the Civil War went on, Lincoln decided the answer was *yes*. As president, he was commander-in-chief of the army and navy—and the Constitution gave him wartime powers against his enemies. He could free the slaves to hurt the Confederacy and help the United States win the war. In his proclamation, he called freeing the slaves "an act of justice."[6] He was glad to be doing a good deed, too.

Lincoln became known as the president who had freed the slaves.

PROCLAMATION OF EMANCIPATION

1861 1863

By the President of the United States of America.

Whereas, On the Twenty-Second day of September, in the year of our Lord one thousand eight hundred and sixty-two, a Proclamation was issued by the President of the United States, containing, among other things the following, to wit:

"That on the first day of January, in the year of our Lord one thousand eight hundred and sixty-three, all persons held as Slaves within any State or designated part of a State, the people whereof shall then be in rebellion against the United States, shall be then, thenceforth, and **FOREVER FREE,** and the EXECUTIVE GOVERNMENT OF THE UNITED STATES, including the military and naval authorities thereof, WILL RECOGNIZE AND MAINTAIN THE FREEDOM of such persons, and will do no act or acts to repress such persons, or any of them, in any efforts they may make for their actual freedom.

"That the Executive will, on the first day of January aforesaid, by proclamation, designate the States and parts of States, if any, in which the people thereof respectively shall then be in rebellion against the United States, and the fact that any State, or the people thereof shall on that day be in good faith represented in the Congress of the United States by members chosen thereto at elections wherein a majority of the qualified voters of such State shall have participated, shall, in the absence of strong countervailing testimony be deemed conclusive evidence that such State and the people thereof are not then in rebellion against the United States."

Now, therefore, I, ABRAHAM LINCOLN, PRESIDENT OF THE UNITED STATES, by virtue of the power in me vested as **Commander-in-Chief of the Army and Navy** of the United States in time of actual armed Rebellion against the authority and government of the United States, and as a fit and necessary war measure for suppressing said Rebellion, do, on this first day of January, in the year of our Lord one thousand eight hundred and sixty-three, and in accordance with my purpose so to do, publicly proclaim for the full period of one hundred days from the day of the first above-mentioned order, and designate, as the States and parts of States wherein the people thereof respectively are this day in rebellion against the United States, the following, to wit: ARKANSAS, TEXAS, LOUISIANA (except the Parishes of St. Bernard, Plaquemines, Jefferson, St. John, St. Charles, St. James, Ascension, Assumption, Terre Bonne, La Fourche, St. Mary, St. Martin, and Orleans, including the City of Orleans), MISSISSIPPI, ALABAMA, FLORIDA, GEORGIA, SOUTH CAROLINA, NORTH CAROLINA, AND VIRGINIA (except the forty-eight counties designated as West Virginia, and also the counties of Berkeley, Accomac, Northampton, Elizabeth City, York, Princess Ann, and Norfolk, including the cities of Norfolk and Portsmouth), and which excepted parts are for the present left precisely as if this Proclamation were not issued.

And by virtue of the power and for the purpose aforesaid, I do order and declare that **ALL PERSONS HELD AS SLAVES** within said designated States and parts of States ARE, AND HENCEFORWARD **SHALL BE FREE!** and that the Executive Government of the United States, including the Military and Naval Authorities thereof, will RECOGNIZE AND MAINTAIN THE FREEDOM of said persons.

And I hereby enjoin upon the people so declared to be free, to abstain from all violence, UNLESS IN NECESSARY SELF-DEFENCE, and I recommend to them that in all cases, when allowed, they LABOR FAITHFULLY FOR REASONABLE WAGES.

And I further declare and make known that such persons of suitable condition will be received into the armed service of the United States, to garrison forts, positions, stations, and other places, and to man vessels of all sorts in said service.

And upon this act, SINCERELY BELIEVED TO BE AN ACT OF JUSTICE, warranted by the Constitution, upon military necessity, I invoke the considerate judgment of mankind, and the gracious favor of ALMIGHTY GOD.

In testimony whereof I have hereunto set my name, and caused the seal of the United States to be affixed.

[L. S.] Done at the CITY OF WASHINGTON, this first day of January, in the year of our Lord one thousand eight hundred and sixty-three, and of the Independence of the United States the eighty-seventh.

By the President.

A. Lincoln

Secretary of State.

LETTING FREEDOM ★RING★

"I never, in my life, felt more certain that I was doing right than I do in signing this paper," Lincoln said of the Emancipation Proclamation.[1]

In truth, issuing the Emancipation Proclamation did not free a single slave. Lincoln said the slaves in the rebelling states were now free. But the Confederates did not

WAITING FOR THE
PROCLAMATION

❖ On December 31, 1862, a large crowd gathered in Boston. They were waiting for midnight, when the Emancipation Proclamation would take effect. Among them were abolitionists William Lloyd Garrison, Harriet Beecher Stowe, and Frederick Douglass, who was weeping with joy.[2] All over, other people waited, too, as in the scene below.

obey Lincoln. Jefferson Davis was their president. Lincoln had no power in the Confederacy.

The proclamation would succeed only if the North won the war and the country was put back together. Then Lincoln would have the power to end slavery throughout the United States.

Lincoln also came up with a plan to deal with slaves in the Border States that were loyal to the Union. He said that the government would pay slave owners if they gave up their slaves.

The Emancipation Proclamation was important because it showed the world that the Civil War was now being fought to end slavery. It also gave hope to millions of black Americans.

Many people cheered when they

▲ soldier reads the Emancipation Proclamation to a group of slaves.

32

heard about it. Horace Greeley, editor of the *New York Tribune*, wrote that it was "the beginning of the new life of the nation."[3] Black Americans were especially happy. "We shout with joy," said Frederick Douglass, an ex-slave who became a leading spokesman for African Americans.[4]

Crowds of people—both black and white—stood outside the White House singing, clapping, and calling out for

Lincoln hoped that the slaves in the South would hear about the Emancipation Proclamation and leave their masters.

Frederick Douglass had risked his life to escape slavery. He was overjoyed when Lincoln issued the Emancipation Proclamation.

the president. They believed the Emancipation Proclamation was a symbol of freedom.

Of course, not everyone was pleased. In the Confederacy, President Jefferson Davis called it one of the most horrible acts in history.[5] Many Northerners were unhappy that the war was now being fought over slavery.

Thousands of former slaves became soldiers for the North.

As a result of the Emancipation Proclamation, thousands of African Americans fled from the South. Both slaves and free blacks headed North to join the Union army. By war's end, nearly 200,000 African

---

◆ BLACK SOLDIERS ◆

Many whites did not like the idea of fighting to free black Americans. "You say you will not fight to free Negroes," said Lincoln. "Some of them seem willing to fight for you."[6]

◈ A Kentucky soldier said he "volunteered to fight to restore the Old Constitution and not to free the Negroes and we are not going to do it."[7]

◈ Some white soldiers were glad blacks were joining the army. "If they can kill rebels I say arm them and set them to shooting," said one soldier from Illinois.[8]

Americans would fight for the Union. Twenty-four would receive the Congressional Medal of Honor.

When Lincoln was elected for another term as president in 1864, he looked old and tired. There were many new lines on his face. The war had been hard on him. He wanted nothing more than peace. Lincoln hoped to "bind up the nation's wounds," he said.[9]

When Confederate general Robert E. Lee surrendered to Union general Ulysses S. Grant on April 9, 1865, the end of the Civil War was finally in sight. The war had lasted four bloody years. More than 600,000 lives had been lost.

At last, 4 million African Americans were now free. That same year, in December, the Thirteenth Amendment

Black Americans in the North cheered for Lincoln's proclamation of freedom. In the South, it took more than two years for all the slaves to find out they were free.

to the U.S. Constitution was passed. Slavery was now against the law in every state of the country.

Five nights after General Lee surrendered, Lincoln was shot. He had been watching a play at Ford's Theater in Washington, D.C. The killer was John Wilkes Booth, an actor who had wanted the South to win the war. He was violently angry with President Lincoln for freeing the slaves. Booth was found and killed twelve days later by federal troops.

Lincoln lived through the night, but he died the next morning. It was April 15, 1865, and he was fifty-six years old. Thousands of people gathered to say good-bye as a train carried Lincoln's body back to Springfield, Illinois.

Finally, the war was over. In 1865, General Lee, below right, surrendered to General Grant at a farmhouse in Virginia.

African Americans were now facing a long struggle to be treated as equal human beings. Issuing the Emancipation Proclamation was only the beginning—but it was a very important beginning.

President Lincoln was very proud of the Emancipation Proclamation. He once said, "If my name ever goes into history, it will be for this act."[11]

"The South is avenged!" shouted Booth after he shot the president.[10]

Lincoln's funeral car paraded through the streets of Washington, D.C.

The Lincoln Memorial in Washington, D.C., honors one of our nation's greatest presidents.

LINCOLN, SLAVERY, ★AND THE★ EMANCIPATION PROCLAMATION TIMELINE

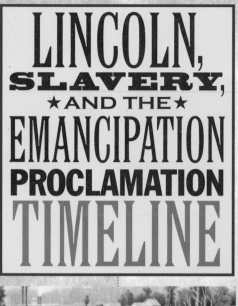

1808
Importing slaves from other countries is outlawed.

1820
Missouri Compromise says Maine will be a free state, Missouri a slave state.

1841
Lincoln returns to his private law practice.

1600s 1700s

1619
African slaves are sold in Jamestown, Virginia.

1662
Virginia law states that slaves from Africa will remain slaves for life.

1774
Northern states begin to abolish slavery.

1793
The cotton gin is invented, giving new life to the slave industry in the South.

1809
Abraham Lincoln is born in a log cabin near Hodgenville, Kentucky.

1818
Ten states allow slavery, and ten do not.

1831
William Lloyd Garrison begins publishing *The Liberator*.

WILLIAM LLOYD GARRISON

1834
Lincoln is elected to the Illinois House of Representatives.

1846
Lincoln is elected to the U.S. House of Representatives.

1850
New law sets stronger punishments for people helping runaway slaves.

40

1858
Lincoln runs for the U.S. Senate against Stephen Douglas, and the two men debate over the issue of slavery. Lincoln loses the election.

1861
Six more Southern states secede, and the Confederate States of America is formed, with Jefferson Davis as president.

1862
Lincoln begins working on the Emancipation Proclamation. He publishes the Preliminary Emancipation Proclamation on September 22.

1865
Confederate general Lee surrenders to Union general Grant.

1865
The rest of the Confederate armies surrender, and the Civil War is over.

Andrew Johnson becomes president.

1800s

1860
Lincoln becomes president of the United States.

South Carolina secedes from the United States.

1861
The Civil War begins, and four more Southern states join the Confederacy.

JEFFERSON DAVIS

1863
Lincoln issues the Emancipation Proclamation on January 1, freeing slaves in the rebelling states.

1864
Lincoln is reelected to a second term as president.

1865
President Lincoln is assassinated.

1865
The Thirteenth Amendment to the Constitution is passed, abolishing slavery in the United States.

abolitionist — Person who wants to put an end to slavery.

auction — A public sale where property is sold to the highest bidder.

confederacy — People or states that have joined together.

Confederate States of America — The eleven southern states that left the United States to become a separate nation: Alabama, Arkansas, Florida, Georgia, Louisiana, Mississippi, North Carolina, South Carolina, Tennessee, Texas, and Virginia.

emancipation — The act of freeing people.

Emancipation Proclamation — A ruling written by President Lincoln that freed all the slaves in the rebelling states.

pioneer — A person who explores unsettled territory.

plantation — A large farm, usually in the South.

preliminary — Before; leading up to the main event or announcement.

proclamation — A public announcement.

secede — To break away from.

union — The uniting of a group of people; during the Civil War, the United States was called the Union.

U.S. Constitution — A paper describing the powers of the government and the rights of the American people. It contains the basic laws of the United States.

Chapter Notes

CHAPTER 1.
Slavery Takes Root

1. Roy P. Basler, ed., *Lincoln: Speeches and Writings 1859–1865* (New Brunswick, N.J.: Rutgers University Press, 1974, p. 585.

2. *The American Presidency: Abraham Lincoln Biography*, <http://gi.grolier.com/presidents/ea/bios/16plinc.html> (October 22, 2003).

3. National Endowment for the Humanities, The Mariners' Museum, *Captive Passage: The Transatlantic Slave Trade and the Making of the Americas*, <http://www.mariner.org/captivepassage/departure/captions/dep013-03.html> (October 22, 2003).

4. *Abstract of the Returns of the Fifth Census* (Washington, D.C.: Duff Gree, 1832), p. 47.

CHAPTER 2.
The Battle Over Slavery

1. William H. Herndon and Jesse W. Weik, *Herndon's Life of Lincoln* (New York: Da Capo Press, 1983), p. 64.

2. *Africans in America: "The Liberator*, 'To the Public,' 1831,"* <http://www.pbs.org/wgbh/aia/part4/4h2928.html> (October 22, 2003).

3. Herndon and Weik, p. 144.

4. Geoffrey C. Ward, *The Civil War: An Illustrated History* (New York: Knopf, 1990), p. 20.

5. William K. Klingaman, *Abraham Lincoln and the Road to Emancipation, 1861–1865* (New York: Viking Penguin, 2001), p. 8.

6. National Center for Public Policy Research, <http://www.nationalcenter.org/HouseDivided.html> (October 22, 2003).

7. Roy P. Basler ed., *The Collected Works of Abraham Lincoln* (New Brunswick, N.J., Rutgers University Press, 1953–1955), vol. 2, p. 461.

CHAPTER 3.
A Nation Torn Apart

1. Ralph Geoffrey Newman, ed., *Abraham Lincoln: His Story in His Own Words* (Garden City, NY: Doubleday & Company, Inc., 1975), p. 61.

2. National Park Service, National UGRR Network to Freedom Program, <http://www.cr.nps.gov/ugrr/learn_a6.htm> (October 22, 2003).

3. William K. Klingaman, *Abraham Lincoln and the Road to Emancipation, 1861–1865* (New York: Viking Penguin, 2001), p. 140.

4. Klingaman, p. 50.

5. Klingaman, p. 139.

6. Stephen B. Oates, *With Malice Toward None: The Life of Abraham Lincoln* (New York: Harper & Row, 1977), p. 309.

7. Shelby Foote, *The Civil War: Fort Sumter to Perryville* (New York: Random House, 1958), p. 705.

8. Klingaman, p. 139.

⟩⟨ Chapter Notes ⟩⟨

CHAPTER 4.
Taking Action

1. John Hope Franklin, *The Emancipation Proclamation* (Garden City, NY: Doubleday & Company, Inc., 1963), p. 35.
2. Franklin, p. 35.
3. *The Emancipation Proclamation*, <http://www.nps.gov/ncro/anti/emancipation.html> (October 22, 2003).
4. William K. Klingaman, *Abraham Lincoln and the Road to Emancipation, 1861–1865* (New York: Viking Penguin, 2001), p. 140.
5. Benjamin Thomas and Harold Hyman, *Stanton: The Life and Times of Lincoln's Secretary of War* (New York: Knopf Books, 1962), p. 239.
6. Abraham Lincoln, *The Emancipation Proclamation, 1863*, <http://usinfo.state.gov/usa/infousa/facts/democrac/24.htm> (March 10, 2004).

CHAPTER 5.
Letting Freedom Ring

1. John Hope Franklin, *The Emancipation Proclamation* (Garden City, NY: Doubleday & Company, Inc., 1963), p. 95.
2. Geoffrey C. Ward, *The Civil War: An Illustrated History* (New York: Knopf, 1990), p. 177.
3. Franklin, p. 62.
4. Stephen B. Oates, *With Malice Toward None: The Life of Abraham Lincoln* (New York: Harper & Row, 1977), p. 320.
5. Stephen B. Oates, *Abraham Lincoln: The Man Behind the Myths* (New York: Harper & Row, 1984), p. 18.
6. Ward, p. 247.
7. James M. McPherson, *For Cause and Comrades: Why Men Fought in the Civil War* (New York: Oxford University Press, 1997), pp. 122–123.
8. McPherson, p. 127.
9. Lincoln's Second Inaugural Address, March 4, 1865, <http://www.ideasign.com/chiliast/pdocs/inaugural/lincoln2.htm> (October 22, 2003).
10. William H. Herndon and Jesse W. Weik, *Herndon's Life of Lincoln* (New York: Da Capo Press, 1983), p. 457.
11. Oates, *With Malice Toward None*, p. 333.

Learn More

Blashfield, Jean F. *Abraham Lincoln*.
Minneapolis, Minn.: Compass Point Books, 2002.

Diouf, Sylviane A. *Growing Up in Slavery*.
Brookfield, Conn.: Millbrook Press, 2001.

Heinrichs. Ann. *The Emancipation Proclamation*.
Minneapolis, Minn.: Compass Point Books, 2002.

Martin, Michael J. *Emancipation Proclamation: Hope of Freedom for the Slaves*. Mankato, Minn.: Bridgestone Books, 2003.

Newman, Shirlee P. *Slavery in the United States*.
New York: Franklin Watts, 2000.

Abolitionism: 1830–1850.
    <http://afroamhistory.about.com/gi/dynamic/offsite.htm?
    site=http%3A%2F%2Fjefferson.village.virginia.
    edu%2Futc%2Fabolitn%2Fabhp.html>

American Experience. The Time of the Lincolns:
Slavery and Freedom.
    <http://www.pbs.org/wgbh/amex/lincolns/slavery/qt_
    aasouth.html>

The Emancipation Proclamation.
    <http://www.nps.gov/ncro/anti/emancipation.html>

 Index

Pages numbers for photographs are in **boldface** type.